Editor-in-Chief and Founder:
  Lyndon H. LaRouche, Jr.
Editorial Board: *Lyndon H. LaRouche, Jr. , Helga
  Zepp-LaRouche, Robert Ingraham, Tony
  Papert, Gerald Rose, Dennis Small, Jeffrey
  Steinberg, William Wertz*
Co-Editors: *Robert Ingraham, Tony Papert*
Managing Editor: *Nancy Spannaus*
Technology: *Marsha Freeman*
Books: *Katherine Notley*
Ebooks: *Richard Burden*
Graphics: *Alan Yue*
Photos: *Stuart Lewis*
Circulation Manager: *Stanley Ezrol*

INTELLIGENCE DIRECTORS
Counterintelligence: *Jeffrey Steinberg, Michele
  Steinberg*
Economics: *John Hoefle, Marcia Merry Baker,
  Paul Gallagher*
History: *Anton Chaitkin*
Ibero-America: *Dennis Small*
Russia and Eastern Europe: *Rachel Douglas*
United States: *Debra Freeman*

INTERNATIONAL BUREAUS
Bogotá: *Miriam Redondo*
Berlin: *Rainer Apel*
Copenhagen: *Tom Gillesberg*
Houston: *Harley Schlanger*
Lima: *Sara Madueño*
Melbourne: *Robert Barwick*
Mexico City: *Gerardo Castilleja Chávez*
New Delhi: *Ramtanu Maitra*
Paris: *Christine Bierre*
Stockholm: *Ulf Sandmark*
United Nations, N.Y.C.: *Leni Rubinstein*
Washington, D.C.: *William Jones*
Wiesbaden: *Göran Haglund*

ON THE WEB
e-mail: eirns@larouchepub.com
www.larouchepub.com
www.executiveintelligencereview.com
www.larouchepub.com/eiw
Webmaster: *John Sigerson*
Assistant Webmaster: *George Hollis*
Editor, Arabic-language edition: *Hussein Askary*

EIR (ISSN 0273-6314) *is published weekly
(50 issues), by EIR News Service, Inc.,
P.O. Box 17390, Washington, D.C. 20041-0390.
(703) 777-9451*

European Headquarters: E.I.R. GmbH, Postfach
Bahnstrasse 9a, D-65205, Wiesbaden, Germany
Tel: 49-611-73650
Homepage: http://www.eirna.com
e-mail: eirna@eirna.com
Director: Georg Neudecker

Montreal, Canada: 514-461-1557

Denmark: EIR - Denmark, Sankt Knuds Vej 11,
basement left, DK-1903 Frederiksberg, Denmark.
Tel.: +45 35 43 60 40, Fax: +45 35 43 87 57. e-mail:
eirdk@hotmail.com.

Mexico City: EIR, Sor Juana Inés de la Cruz 242-2
Col. Agricultura C.P. 11360
Delegación M. Hidalgo, México D.F.
Tel. (5525) 5318-2301
eirmexico@gmail.com

Canada Post Publication Sales Agreement
#40683579

Postmaster: Send all address changes to *EIR*, P.O.
Box 17390, Washington, D.C. 20041-0390.

Signed articles in *EIR* represent the views of the
authors, and not necessarily those of the Editorial
Board.

Four New Laws

EIR Contents

www.larouchepub.com Volume 43, Number 32, August 5, 2016

Cover This Week

Mars Rover, Curiosity

NASA

I. LaRouche's Four Laws

THE NEW PRESIDENCY

It Begins with LaRouche's 'Four Laws'

by Michael G. Steger

This article is the first in a series of writings which will be presented by the LaRouche PAC National Policy Committee, in direct collaboration with Lyndon La-Rouche, as part of his campaign to create a New Presidency over the coming 100 days.

August 2—Over the last five weeks the world has changed. Events combined with willful interventions, especially those of Vladimir Putin, have created a new global dynamic and transformed the potential for real and total victory in the immediate period ahead. Success now depends first on the adoption of LaRouche's 'Four New Laws,' a policy set forth in 2014 in his "The Four New Laws to Save the U.S.A. Now!," but long-term success requires more than simple adoption of necessary policies, even ones as necessary as Glass-Steagall and Federal Credit for scientific advancement.

As LaRouche states in "The Four New Laws,"

"In principle, without a Presidency suited to remove and dump the worst effects felt presently, those created presently by the Bush-Cheney and Obama Presidencies, the United States were soon finished, beginning with the mass-death of the U.S. population under the Obama Administration's recent and now accelerated policies of practice."

And then later,

"A chain-reaction collapse, to this effect, is already accelerating with an effect on the money-systems of the nations of that region. The present acceleration of a 'Bail-in' policy throughout the trans-Atlantic region, as underway now, means mass-death suddenly hitting the populations of all nations within that trans-Atlantic region: whether directly, or by 'overflow.'"

This systemic crisis requires not just a set of policies, but a New Presidency, one based on a citizenry with a higher devotion, one beyond mere electoral politics, one similar to that of Benjamin Franklin, George Washington, and Alexander Hamilton. It requires a commitment to the creation of a new nation, of a new United States, and of a world that has never existed before—a world now more possible than ever, and a world that now lies in our hands whether it comes to be, or we fall short.

The Five Weeks

Now consider the rapid developments of the last five weeks:

The British-exit (Brexit) vote from the European Union on June 24, exposed as if suddenly, for all the world to see, the rotting core of the trans-Atlantic system. This rebellion among British voters was the direct prelude to the Helga Zepp-LaRouche-hosted Schiller Institute conference in Berlin that same weekend, an event uniquely focused on the fulfillment of the new world system now coming into being throughout Eurasia and inspired by the ideas of Lyndon LaRouche.

Within days successive upheavals poured forth. The NATO summit in Warsaw, hoping to target Russia for greater war, instead only exposed growing discord among the European nations. Japan rejected any further commitment to British financial insanity, and in fact moved closer to Russia and China, as did the Philippines, ignoring Obama's command for conflict in the South China Sea. Terrorist attacks, spawned by the on-going the illegal U.S./British wars in Iraq, Libya, Syria and Yemen, have targeted cities in France and Germany weekly, if not daily, with no end in sight under the current policies. Underlying all of this political upheaval, there is the ongoing public panic over the banking collapse in Italy, Germany, and London, threatening that very sudden wipe-out of the nations of the trans-Atlantic that Lyndon LaRouche had forewarned of in 2014.

In the context of this political and cultural breakdown in the trans-Atlantic region, there has been a surge of the policies and initiatives of the LaRouche organization. The Chilcot Inquiry was finally released in London after seven long years of review, declaring the Queen's war in Iraq—a war forced through by Tony Blair and George W. Bush—to be illegal and a direct attack on the United Nations and international law, crimes tantamount to those of the Nazis. In the United States, the "28 pages" of the Joint Congressional Inquiry into 9/11 were released after 14 years, exposing the fraud of both the Bush and Obama administrations for their explicit cover-up of the British-Saudi direction of the 9/11 attacks, as well as their subsequent drive for world war through geopolitical criminal intent.

The Glass-Steagall act, the very death-knell of Wall Street's and London's criminal fraud, then found its way into both the Republican and Democratic Party's platforms, not because of the clown-shows of the joke-candidates, but because of the deeply held recognition by the broad majority of the American people, that the last fifteen years of mass-death policy in the United States is undeniably tied to the policies of Wall Street.

And now, just five weeks later, resolving as if upwards with much more to come, the near-coup in Turkey and subsequent policy changes threaten to end the last two centuries of geopolitical attempts to control Asia, as Turkey now turns closer to both Putin's Russia and China's New Silk Road policy, and away from the trans-Atlantic commitment to world war. Then comes the news of the encirclement of Aleppo, again by Putin's Russian along with Syrian forces, indicating a possible near-term end, not just to the Syrian conflict which was intended as a pre-emption toward nuclear war against Russia and China by the British-backed Obama regime, but which now, with the crisis nearly resolved, portends the end of the era of British geopolitics itself. Vladimir Putin and China's New Silk Road are winning; Obama and the British are losing.

Yet there is more, and perhaps more to come, beginning with the participation by Helga Zepp-LaRouche in the international T20 summit in Beijing at the end of July, a preliminary discussion of leading figures for the upcoming G20 summit in September. The United Nations General Assembly will also meet in September, merely a year since Vladimir Putin's call for a new allied force against terrorism, and both events will be key international forums to build upon the LaRouche-inspired new paradigm.

As Helga Zepp-LaRouche said recently, "The Erinyes' dreadful dance has been unleashed!" and one can almost hear the panicked howling and screaming inside the corridors of power on Wall Street and in London, even from the batty Queen herself.

The Four Laws

On June 8, 2014, Lyndon LaRouche issued a statement, titled "The Four New Laws to Save the U.S.A. Now! Not an Option: an Immediate Necessity."

In his statement of 'The Four New Laws,' Mr. LaRouche defines a solution to the current global economic and financial, general breakdown crisis, but he also defines more. He presents an economic and scientific policy which is coherent with the actual creative nature of the human species, and one which, if adopted, will unleash a Renaissance in human advancement for the coming century, and beyond.

There is no substitute for reading, and re-reading, the entirety of Mr. LaRouche's statement, but we will present here a brief truncated synopsis of the immediate steps to be taken to address the ongoing general breakdown crisis of the trans-Atlantic system. This is the starting point for a successful New Presidency:

1. The immediate re-enactment of the Glass-Steagall law instituted by U.S. President Franklin D. Roosevelt, without modification, as to principle of action.
2. A return to a system of top-down, and thoroughly so defined, as National Banking. The precedents for this shall be taken from the banking-and-credit system established by Alexander Hamilton, as well as Abraham Lincoln's action of creating a national currency ("Greenbacks"), under Presidential authority.
3. The deployment of a new Federal Credit system to generate high-productivity trends in improvements

of employment, with the accompanying intention to increase the physical-economic productivity, and the standard of living of the persons and households of the United States. An increase in productive employment, as accomplished under Franklin Roosevelt, must reflect an increase in real productivity, coherent with an increase in energy-flux density in the nation's economic practice.

4. The adoption of a "Fusion-Driver 'Crash Program.'" Real economics is grounded in the essential distinction of man from all lower forms of life. A Fusion Crash Program, today subsuming a return to Krafft Ehricke's vision for the U.S. Space Program, is a commitment to mankind's future.

The Deeper Issue

However, only a quality of thinking similar to that of a creative scientist, such as Einstein, or the conductor Wilhelm Furtwängler, will have the powers necessary to grasp the underlying causal force of the recent international developments, as well as the sufficient quality of response found in the very essence of LaRouche's Four New Laws. This scientific quality is best expressed as one's own commitment to the unbounded future of the human species.

Not the future of the reductionist's space and time, or even space-time, but rather a future governed by musical genius, which looks to engender in the mind of an audience the necessary and sufficient powers of thought which approximate mankind's unlimited future, thus unfolding a clarity of resolute action as if backwards into the present crisis from the living future.

Shakespeare's case of Hamlet provides a relevant negative proof of such powers of the human mind. Any honest person must ask themselves, not "For whom will I vote?," but rather, "Will I exist as an efficient actor on the stage of history?" As Lyndon LaRouche stated on July 31, 2016, "I am not running for President, but I am certainly intending to affect the shaping of the government of the United States in the coming period."

Now consider this aspect of his thinking in the concluding section of that June, 2014 report,

"For example: 'time' and 'space' do not actually exist as a set of metrical principles of the Solar system; their only admissible employment for purposes of communication is essentially nominal presumption. Since competent science for today can be expressed only in terms of the unique characteristic of the human species' role within the known aspects of the universe, the human principle is the only true principle known to us for practice: the notions of space and time are merely useful imageries."

And then later,

"Man is mankind's only true measure of the history of our Solar system, and what reposes within it. That is the same thing, as the most honored meaning and endless achievement of the human species, now within nearby Solar space, heading upward to mastery over the Sun and its Solar system, the one discovered (uniquely, as a matter of fact), by Johannes Kepler."

The danger lies, thus, not in the seeming chaos of world events, as the typical man-on-the-street perceives the unfolding crisis, but in the insufficient commitment towards the upward nature of mankind, as presented in LaRouche's Four New Laws. For at such a moment when LaRouche's ideas are now more influential within the broader culture of the human species, and while the contrary deceits of Zeusian imperial dictates of population reduction, war, and economic fraud face their perilous collapse, the very nature of the human mind itself is the higher compositional modality by which we act upon the universe-at-large to revolutionary effect.

What is urgent is the requisite creative pre-emptive action, rather than the repeated failures derived from Newton's systemic fraud of action-reaction—a fraud that predominates in the neurotic impulses of the political and financial class of the trans-Atlantic today, and a fraud that Einstein so brilliantly exposed. Such pre-emptive action, as required by LaRouche's Four New Laws, is the very foundation for the preliminary steps by which we eliminate the unnecessary burdens and debts of this failed system.

But, can one hear the new theme, perhaps as if by the anticipated entrance of a soaring section of woodwinds high above the orchestra in highest register? For such anticipation is as if a gift brought unexpectedly by a long-past dear friend from what is the yet undetermined future, which is then given on behalf of our present's passing, only to become our future's most profound present.

Dante's *Divine Comedy*, and Brunelleschi's creation of the Italian Renaissance, were no less.

So must the New Presidency, and its citizenry, become.

Man's Unique Nature

by Tony Papert

July 28—Only the adoption of Lyndon LaRouche's June 8, 2014 "Four New Laws to Save the U.S.A. Now," can save the trans-Atlantic region from a "general, physical-economic chain-reaction breakdown-crisis." If you intend to be anything more than a mere bystander, or worse, in this onrushing crisis, you must read and understand the Four Laws.

What I hope to do here is to improve your insight, if possible, into the great premise underlying LaRouche's Four Laws. That premise, as he makes clear, is the totally unique nature of the human species in the entire universe. Only man creates new forms of existence never seen before and otherwise impossible. Only man creates the future; only man creates the future existence of humanity; and only man creates human creativity itself.

This true human nature is most accessible to visionary scientists,— and there is no true scientist who is not a visionary.

Space pioneer Krafft A. Ehricke, who became a close co-worker with Lyndon and Helga LaRouche during the 1980s, was such a visionary scientist. Writing in the dark days of the early 1950s (in the first volume of his work, *Space Flight*), he reached back through millions of years of evolution to recall "the enormous effort" which "waterborne life" had undertaken "to adapt itself to existence on land." He likened that to man's stepping out into space,— not through biological evolution, but through the new quality of the human mind.

Thoughts like these of Ehricke's permeated the space pioneers,— it is known that Wernher von Braun compared Neil Armstrong's stepping onto the surface of the moon, with that "enormous

A Saturn V (500-Foot Test Vehicle) at Pad 39A at dawn in the Summer of 1966.

NASA

effort" through which life moved from the ocean onto the land.

In a magnificent work written in 1966, which looked back from the year 2000 on what he foresaw would be man's progress in space since 1966, Krafft Ehricke said that now (in 2000) an average of two flights per month are taking off from earth for other parts of the solar system,— plus incomparably more satellite and moon-launches. Most of the spaceships travelling through solar space are powered by controlled fusion using the deuterium-helium-3 reaction. Ehricke does not simply name this reaction; he goes into great detail about both the reaction itself, and how it can be controlled and used for a rocket engine. But he notes that the deuterium-helium-3 reaction will not hold first place for long,—because already man is moving toward mastery of matter-antimatter reactions.

In a memorable passage, Ehricke recalls how mankind had freed itself from the death-cult of the 20th Century, to embrace its new-found freedom:

We, in the year 2000, look back at the twentieth century as the years in which the new era was finally born after centuries of incubation in the minds and hearts of great men and women of many nations. The twentieth century is the gulf which separates the last century of the old era and the first century of the new one in which values, outlooks and frames of reference are quite different. The hour of birth, be it of a life or of an era, is the hour of truth in which pain, doubt and fear challenge, and the intensity of their onslaught causes the compensating forces of strength, confidence and bravery to rise to rare peaks of intensity and power. The world seems to break apart under the agony of this unmerciful confrontation of the old and the new. The great symbols of the space age, namely, rocket technology, nuclear technology and modern electronic technology were born in the dark days of World War II. But, since war can never bear peace, the rockets remained missiles, the nuclear devices remained bombs and the radar did not cease to be the ear which was anxiously listening for the signal of death from the hostile world of "the other side." The past was lost, the future not yet won; and mankind shivered in the feverish chill of hostility, hatred and death-fear unleashed in the succession of wars and confrontations.

These were the realities.

Throughout those years, a small group of people of many nationalities, while facing those realities, refused to surrender their vision of missiles-turned-spacecraft, of nuclear power becoming a means of propelling space vehicles to other worlds and of radar waves reporting exciting discoveries from deep space. What they suggested seemed at first impractical, inconsequential and without utility or payoff. But we now know that they had built their case on the solid foundations of long-range logic and realism .... Space became a very real challenge to man; and there was no way back to the old days. There never is. ["Solar Transportation." American Astronautical Society Science and Technology Series, vol. 10, *Space Age in Fiscal Year 2001*, An American Astronautical Society Publication, 1967, p. 164]

Let us conclude with Krafft's retelling of the beginning of the space age with the first successful launch of the first cosmic rocket, the German A-4, later called the V-2, on October 3, 1942.

Those were the "wild west" days of rocketry and space flight. You didn't have to be miles away. You could almost stand beside the rocket, and I was on the roof of one of those high-rise buildings, actually looking down to the launch complex, just a few hundred meters distance. And then came the countdown and ignition. The system lifted off with a roar. It lifted up straight,

and, of course, we all screamed with delight. It hadn't exploded on the launch complex. The guidance system seemed to work... it looked like a fiery sword going into the sky. Then came the enormous roar—the whole sky seemed to vibrate. This kind of unearthly roaring sound was something human ears had never heard [before].

You know, it's very hard to describe what you feel when you stand on the threshold of a whole new era, of a whole new age that you know will be coming. It's like those people must have felt—Columbus or Magellan—that for the first time, saw entire new worlds, and knew the world would never be the same after this... This is the feeling many of us had.

For me, it was absolutely overwhelming. I almost fell off the roof, I was so excited.

When we came down together we congratulated ourselves. We knew the Space Age had begun and Dr. Dornberger made a very moving speech at the time, and said, "Well, this is the key to the universe. This is the first day of the Space Age." [Marsha Freeman, *Krafft Ehricke's Extraterrestrial Imperative*, Apogee Books, 2008, p. 16]

LaRouche on Albert Einstein

Lyndon LaRouche spoke to the following effect in a discussion with associates on July 31.

Now, the question is, the problem is,— and this is a problem that very few people in the United States today in particular, as well as in Europe,— know yet. They don't know what Einstein knew; what Einstein knew in his sort of second incarnation, when his continuing work was producing more and more insight into the whole question of what the nature of mankind is.

Now, the point is, people talk about mankind as being a person which is made in terms of man as such, but that is not true. The truth of the matter is that the human being who is worth anything, has a power of creativity which goes beyond anything that any individual person by themselves could ever accomplish. In other words, there is no such thing as a typical person. A typical person does not exist. And it shouldn't exist. It's a good idea that it should not exist.

Because the question is, what is mankind capable of doing, that mankind has otherwise never been able to do? And the point is that you don't win something by what you do,— you have to *create, in yourself* a commitment to a kind of development of the population around us. And that is what is the power.

Practical people are not worth anything. They're not capable of understanding any of this. But the power of creativity,— which actually, Krafft Ehricke already understood in his own way,— that's it: Mankind is something which lies in the spiritual character of the human species, per capita. That power, as it's developed, as it's presented, presents man with a new vision of mankind,— just as Einstein, in his greatest achievements, discovered the future of humanity, way beyond the type that any individual person as such was able to represent.

And so this is the issue. You have to understand that mankind is not the "El Cheapo" element that most people think he is. And it is that power, that power of creativity, which is based on the *will*, the will like an Einstein will, to create the Universe, and to rebuild the Universe on a higher basis. Without that, we are not complete.

OK, that much said...

Michael Steger: Your presidential-like campaign intervention around the *Four Laws* has produced something even more powerful today, if we recognize the shift that's taken place.

Lyndon LaRouche: Yes: I would say I've done this thing, of course, naturally, and presented it repeatedly over time. But when you look at it from the standpoint of the Einstein standpoint, the reference to Einstein as a point of reference on what mankind's achievements can be: That is really what is most important. You have to realize that people like Helga and me, and Krafft Ehricke and so forth,— we were all part of a group of people who came together, and joined ourselves with a mutual effort, to provide a full investment in what the potentiality is, for what mankind is.

Now, the point is that Krafft Ehricke, contrary to some people, knew, and told my wife Helga, that he was aware of the fact of his death, the nature of his own death. And therefore he was concerned about how we deal with this thing. And that's what we all have to do now. Because inherently the human species is not a practical thing; practical people are sick people, and therefore you want to have people be able, as Krafft Ehricke had yearned, to realize what could have been, between his fate as a sick person in that condition, and the fact that he wished to be able to continue his work for the rest of mankind.

And this should force people who are serious, to say: What is it that we have to assure to our fellow citizens, which is necessary that mankind in being, has the power to create the kind of forces that Einstein's principle represents?

AGONY OF CONFRONTATION BETWEEN OLD AND NEW

The New World Imperative

by Robert Ingraham

July 30—On July 21, 1969, Neil Armstrong became the first member of the human species to set foot on another celestial body. This action portended a new future for humanity, new challenges, new discoveries, and an enhancement of the human identity. None of this happened. That mission was willfully abandoned, and to this day, the possibilities of July 21, 1969 remain an unrealized potential.

Instead, there exists in our current trans-Atlantic culture a pernicious mental disease, one which has been intensively cultivated by the U.S. Federal Bureau of Investigation and other oligarchical entities. It is a psychological malady, wherein an individual defines his or her sense of identity by what one opposes, what one is "against."

Human progress has never been realized through such a *Hobbesian* outlook. The human species would have died out long ago if our ancestors had acted solely on the basis of such a stunted identity. One of the great accomplishments of the 1861-1865 American Civil War was the abolition of slavery. But was the species-character of that war defined as being merely *against* slavery? A reflective rereading of Abraham Lincoln's Gettysburg Address and his Second Inaugural Address shows otherwise.

Rather, we find in mankind's destiny a continuous impulse—to conquer new realms of scientific and artistic insight; to expand our understanding of the universe and the role our species plays therein; to increase the

NASA

Two astronaut mission specialists of Space Shuttle Atlantis on an eight-hour space walk, as they continued repairs and improvements to the Hubble Space Telescope on May 17, 2009, extending Hubble's life well into the present decade.

productive power of the human race, here on earth and ultimately in the heavens.

Krafft Ehricke, the great genius of America's Apollo Space Program, understood this necessary quality of human existence, and he named it the "Extraterrestrial Imperative." This imperative derives not merely from any practical need to explore and colonize "outer space," for the purpose of finding minerals, raw materials, or simply living quarters for future human population growth. Although many of these benefits might prove useful to future generations, the primary stimulus is to be found, not in merely practical concerns, but in mankind's unceasing mission to understand, in ever greater perfection, the lawful nature of the universe, and the increasing of humanity's productive power over both the terrestrial and extraterrestrial environment.

In a book titled **Space Flight**, published in 1960, in Chapter One, "Prelude to Space Flight," Ehricke says the following:

> To expand to the limits of the inhabitable world appears to be life's most powerful impulse ...
>
> Man's longing for the ability to exist in the extraterrestrial realm must have been born along with his first capacity to be impressed by the starry sky, long before recorded history. With the development of the astral religions, he entered into a personal relationship with the extraterrestrial world and developed the foundations of human morality. This forever correlated in his mind the star-filled universe with his highest philosophical and religious concepts. Celestial events, such as eclipses and the appearance of comets, became of great significance for good or bad. A star announced the birth of Christ to the world; ...
>
> Astronomy is the oldest of the sciences, ... the challenge of space, in whichever form it happened to be understood, ultimately became a powerful stimulus to man's scientific curiosity.

All human progress has arisen from such vision and such prompting, as Ehricke discusses here. In this work, we will look at an earlier epoch in human development, an earlier era of crisis and challenge—and one of equally profound import—that is, the greatly misunderstood discovery and exploration of the **New World** in the late 15th and early 16th Centuries.

I. Florence

Between June of 1502 and March of 1503, while in the employment of Cesare Borgia,[1] Leonardo da Vinci traveled extensively along the route of the Arno River in Tuscany, examining its tributaries, and mapping the headwaters of the river in the Apennine Mountains. Leonardo began to explore the economic benefits to be achieved by controlling the flow of the Arno. The maps which Leonardo later drew in 1503 and 1504 clearly show the design for a number of locks, enabling the water flow of the Arno to be utilized for mills, flood control, irrigation, and increased food production.

But in the course of these labors, a new idea emerged. From October, 1502 to January, 1503 Leonardo was joined, in Borgia's army, by Niccolo Machiavelli who was there as the official envoy of the Florentine government. Machiavelli and da Vinci were already known to each other from at least 1501, when it was Machiavelli who secured a position for Leonardo with Cesare Borgia.

It is now not possible to know what discussions took place between the two men as they traveled with Borgia's army, but what is known is that two months after returning to Florence, Machiavelli presented a plan to the Florentine government, designed by da Vinci, for the diversion of the Arno River. In this plan a new component was added—the construction of a second canal which would transform Florence into a seaport, capable of handling the type of ships which were then beginning the exploration of the Western Hemisphere.

Mundus Novus

To understand the context within which the Leonardo/Machiavelli project was advanced, it is necessary to understand the culture-shattering events which were impacting Florence at that time. In December of 1502, a manuscript had appeared in Florence, and within weeks it became widely circulated among leaders in the city. Although it was not authored by him, the manuscript was based on a, now lost, letter, written by Amerigo Vespucci (1454-1512) to Lorenzo di Pierfrancesco de' Medici,[2] describing the former's Third Voyage across the Atlantic into the western hemisphere. A Frenchman, Giovanni Giocondo, translated the manuscript from the Italian into Latin, elaborating and expanding it, and published it in 1503, under Vespucci's name, giving it the title of **Mundus Novus** (The New World).

It begins with these words:

---

1. Cesare and Lucrezia Borgia were the great enemies of Venice and the old Roman black nobility, as well as the allies of Machiavelli, including Lucrezia's role in Ferrara during the war of the League of Cambrai against Venice in 1508. All quotes by Amerigo Vespucci are taken from {Letters From A New World,} edited by Luciano Formisano, transl. David Jacobson, (New York: Marsilio, 1992.)

2. Lorenzo di Pierfrancesco (1463-1503), a cousin of Lorenzo the Magnificent, was a leader of the junior (Popolano) branch of the Medici family. He was also, for many years, the patron and backer of both Vespucci and Machiavelli.

In days past I have written to you (Lorenzo di Pierfrancesco) at some length concerning my return from those new regions which we discovered and explored with the fleet ..., and which we can rightly call the *New World* since our ancestors had no knowledge of them, and it will be a matter wholly new to all those who hear about them. We learned that this land is not an island but a continent... Most of our ancient authorities assert that there is no continent south of the equator, but merely the sea... but this last voyage of mine has demonstrated that this opinion is false and contradicts all truth, since I have discovered a continent in those southern regions.

Consider the following chronology:

In 1502 Vespucci's letter to Lorenzo di Pierfrancesco, announcing that he had discovered a new continent, reaches Florence, is immediately circulated in manuscript form and communicated to the government. The *Signoria* (the Florentine government) declares a national holiday to celebrate the news, and for three days festivities are conducted in front of the Vespucci home!

At this time, Leonardo da Vinci, working as Borgia's engineer, makes several trips to explore the headwaters of the Arno River.

In the Winter and Spring of 1503, manuscripts of the **Mundus Novus** circulate widely in Florence, just as both Machiavelli and Leonardo return to Florence from Borgia's army. The manuscripts create a sensation and are rapidly republished in Lisbon, Cologne, Strasbourg, Antwerp, Venice, Augsburg, and other cities.

Throughout 1503 and into 1504, Leonardo continues to improve his designs. Several of his mature

This aerial map of the Arno Valley was drawn by a young Leonardo da Vinci in about 1473, and shows his early interest in hydrodynamics. It is a harbinger of the later Arno project. Below, left to right: Leonardo da Vinci, Niccolò Machiavelli.

sketches from that period are now in the *Codex Madrid* and the Windsor Royal Library, and show detailed plans that would have made the Arno navigable and thereby transformed Florence into a seaport.

In 1504 Machiavelli begins a correspondence with Bartolomeo Vespucci, nephew of Amerigo and a professor of Astronomy at the University of Padua, on the subject of astronomy. About this time Leonardo's notebooks begin to include numerous references to writings and maps on astronomy and cosmography. Also in Leonardo's notebooks, from this period, are studies in measuring longitude, so as to enable navigators to make accurate astronomical readings of a ship's location. This is the exact problem that Amerigo Vespucci worked on during his voyages to South America.

Also in 1504, Machiavelli's close ally, Piero Soderini (1452-1522), receives six letters from his lifelong friend Vespucci, describing his four voyages.

These letters are immediately published and widely circulated.

In the summer of 1504, Machiavelli, this time with the strong backing of Soderini, succeeds in obtaining the backing of the *Signoria* for the Arno Project.

II. Earlier Origins

In presenting the 1502-1504 developments from Florence in the above paragraphs, we are, of course, discussing events which took place ten or more years after Christopher Columbus sailed westward. We shall return to the subject of Columbus later, but to tell this story properly, we must first turn our attention to an era two generations earlier, to the time of Filippo Brunelleschi (1377-1446) and his immediate successors.

Much has been written concerning Brunelleschi's leadership in the construction of the great Dome of the Florence Cathedral (*Cattedrale di Santa Maria del Fiore*). All that will be stated here is that, in his work from 1420 to 1436, culminating in the successful completion of the Dome, there are two points which need to be made: The first is that, in the process of designing and building the Dome, Brunelleschi broke all of the existing rules of mathematics and architecture; second, Brunelleschi not only discovered previously undiscovered principles which allowed him to succeed, but, more importantly, he demonstrated that the principles which permeate the universe are *knowable* to man.

In one poetic sonnet which he wrote, defending his methods against a critic, Brunelleschi wrote:

When hope is given to us by Heaven,
O you ridiculous-looking beast,
We rise above corruptible matter
And gain the strength of clearest sight.
A fool will lose what hope he has,
For all experience disappoints him.
For wise men nothing that exists
Remains unseen; they do not share
The idle dreams of would-be scholars.
Only the artist, not the fool
Discovers that which nature hides.
Therefore untangle the web of your verses,
Lest they strike sour notes in the dance
When your "impossible" comes to pass.

In one, staggering and seemingly miraculous ac-

complishment, Brunelleschi destroyed the world of medieval Aristotelian scholasticism and demonstrated the coherence of physical space and universal laws with the creative nature of the human mind. Modern physical science began.

Brunelleschi, Toscanelli, and Cusa

The young Paolo dal Pozzo Toscanelli (1397-1482) met and became friends with Brunelleschi around 1425, when Toscanelli was 28 and Brunelleschi was 48. By the 1430s, Toscanelli was already the leading mathematician and cartographer in Florence. The two men collaborated and worked together for two decades, precisely during the time period when Brunelleschi was directing the construction of the Dome, and it was Toscanelli who, later in 1475, designed and installed the *gnomon* in the Lantern of the Florence Cathedral, of which more will be said later in this work.

Toscanelli was also the life-long friend—some sources say closest friend—of Nicholas of Cusa (1401-1464), since their time together as students at the University of Padua, as early as 1417. The two men shared lodgings together, and they both studied mathematics under Prodocimo de' Beldomandi. Cusa would later dedicate two of his writings to Toscanelli, and his famous work *De quadratura circuli*, "On Squaring the Circle," written in 1458, is set as a dialogue between the two of them. Cusa and Toscanelli collaborated intimately in bringing into existence the 1439 Council of Florence, which convened only three years after Brunelleschi's completion of the Dome on the Cathedral of *Santa Maria del Fiore*, and, in 1464 Toscanelli would attend Cusa at his death-bed and become the executor of his last will and testament.

The Vespucci Family

After the death of Nicholas of Cusa, it was Giorgio Antonio Vespucci (1434-1514), the uncle of Amerigo Vespucci, who became Toscanelli's closest scientific collaborator. Together, the two men would create an intellectual study group at the Abbey of Settimo, in Florence.

In 1453 Giorgio Antonio established a school for personally-selected pupils at the monastery of San Marco, and educated them in a curriculum of mathematics, astronomy, cosmography, Dante, Petrarch, Plato, Cicero, Heraclitus, and Livy. Among his pupils were his nephew Amerigo, and the future *Gonfalonier*[3]

---
3. Essentially, President of the Florentine Republic.

of the Florentine Republic—and political partner of Machiavelli—Piero Soderini.

From among Giorgio Antonio's pupils, Toscanelli chose a smaller number to personally tutor. These included Lorenzo di Pierfrancesco de' Medici, Machiavelli's patron in 1498, and also Amerigo Vespucci, who ended up studying under Toscanelli for more than ten years. Following Toscanelli's death in 1482, Amerigo was considered the greatest cosmographer and mapmaker in Florence, and the recognized successor to Toscanelli in those fields.

Among the closest friends of Amerigo's parents was Bernardo Machiavelli, the father of Niccolo, and it seems apodictical that Niccolo and Amerigo must have known each other, given the intimacy of their families, and the close proximity of the two households, in the same neighborhood.

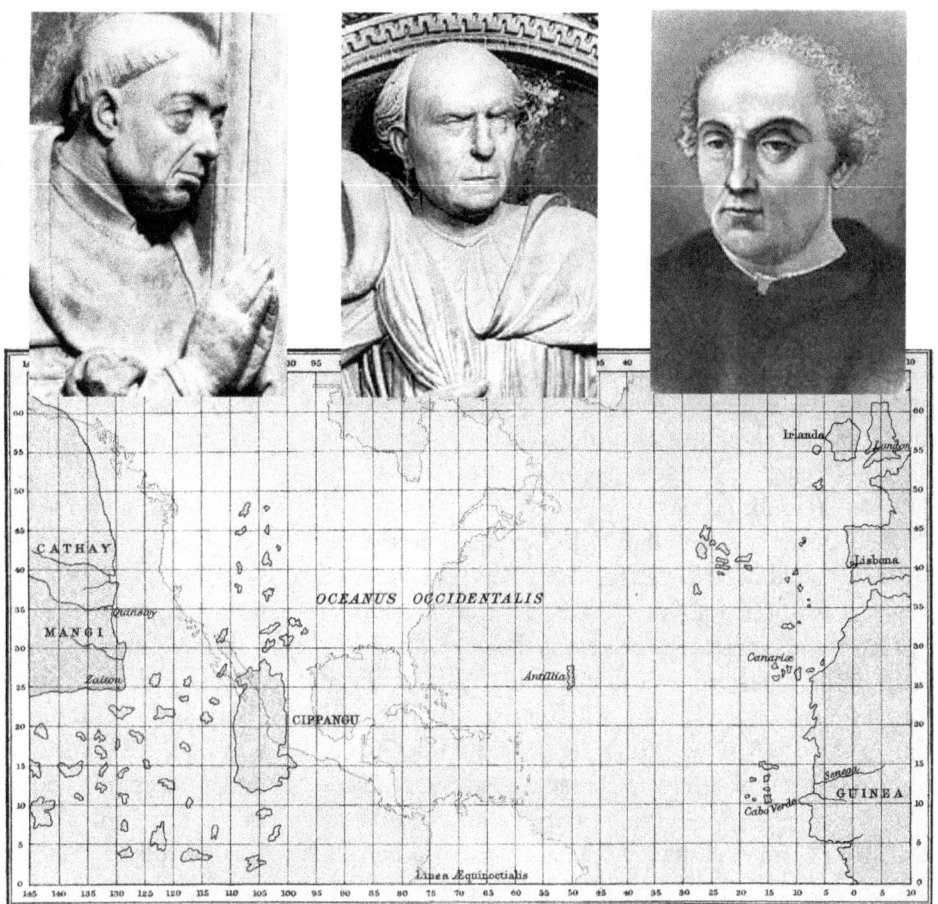

Toscanelli's map, produced in 1474. The correct outline of North America is shown in light blue tint. Above, left to right: Cardinal Nicholas of Cusa, Filippo Brunelleschi, and Paolo dal Pozzo Toscanelli.

In 1498, another of Amerigo's uncles, Guido Antonio Vespucci—together with Lorenzo di Pierfrancesco—played the key role in elevating the previously obscure Niccolo Machiavelli to the post of Second Chancellor of the Florentine Republic.

III. Cristoforo Colombo

The correspondence between Christopher Columbus and Toscanelli, and the map which Toscanelli supplied to Columbus, are both now widely recognized as matters of fact, and the Toscanelli-Columbus connection is firmly established.

But there is a lot more to this story than simply one letter and one map.

Most histories that examine the beginnings of European oceanic exploration begin with a discussion of the role of Henry the Navigator (1394-1460), the invention of the *Caravel*, and Portugal's early leadership in sailing into the Atlantic Ocean. In 1470, when Toscanelli first put forward his idea for sailing westward across the Atlantic, this was done in a proposal to the Portuguese King Afonso V, who rejected it. And in the 1480s when Columbus took up this project, he looked to Portugal as the natural sponsor, but once again the Portuguese king, this time John II, turned him down, both in 1485 and 1488.

The Scientific Challenge of Navigation

Initially, several islands located hundreds of miles west of the Iberian Peninsula, including the Azores, and Madeira, were discovered (or re-discovered) by seamen in the employ of Henry the Navigator, but after his death the Portuguese abandoned all efforts to sail westward and spent the next forty years sailing along the coast of Africa, until they rounded the Cape of Good Hope in 1498.

The difficulty in sailing westward was one of essentially "sailing into the unknown." The existence of the Azores and other islands was already known before the Portuguese landed on them. They were shown on many ancient maps. In addition, fishing boats and other vessels had come across them from time to time. To go beyond the Azores, however, to sail 1,000 or more miles into the ocean where there was no prior historical record of such a voyage,—certainly this would test the courage of everyone involved. What was also clear was that such a project could not hope to succeed unless it utilized the most advanced knowledge in astronomy, cartography, and navigation, as well as the best available technology. In this sense, the requirements were no different than the voyage and return home of the Apollo 11 mission to the moon.

For example, Columbus' 1492 expedition of three ships included two *caravels* and one *carrick*. The caravel was developed about 1450, under the sponsorship of Henry the Navigator, and it was the first ship which allowed the possibility of sailing into the open ocean. The more advanced carrick, which bore many similarities to the *Junk* of the Ming Dynasty, was developed toward the end of the 15th Century, and it was the carrick which made possible global exploration.[4] When Vasco da Gama rounded Africa, it was in a carrick; when Jacques Cartier explored the Saint Lawrence River, it was in a carrick, and when Magellan circumnavigated the globe, it was in a carrick. The carrick was the Saturn V Rocket of its day.

How Do You Know Where You Are?

Moving along vast distances on the surface of a globe, while both that globe, the sun around which it orbits, and all of the stars in heaven are also moving, at different speeds and in different directions, poses enormous problems for navigating over open water.

Prior to the invention of the quadrant and the sextant, sea travel was dependent on two pieces of technology: the compass and the astrolabe. The compass gave direction, and the astrolabe measured the angle between the horizon and the Pole Star (among other functions), and allowed navigators to roughly determine the latitude of one's position. These tools were useful, but the astrolabe was imprecise, and it also did not solve the

problem of determining longitude. Without being able to fix one's longitudinal position, there is no way to tell exactly where you are.[5] You could be hundreds of miles, or more, east or west of your desired position.

The ability to navigate precisely was a huge problem that many of the Arab navigators of the Middle Ages had struggled with, and it was the great Arab astronomer and musical instrument maker al-Zarqali (Abu Is aq Ibrahim ibn Yahya al-Naqqash al-Zarqali), who, in the 11th Century, developed an extremely precise method to compute the "positions of the celestial bodies" on any given day of the year and to predict the movement of the planets relative to the fixed stars. In the 12th Century al-Zarqali's computations were translated into Latin and published as the *Tables of Toledo*, becoming the most widely used navigational tool.

Then, in the 13th Century, King Alfonso X of Castile (Alfonso the Wise) had all of al-Zarqali's works translated into Spanish. These were then published under the name "Libros de las laminas de los planetas" (Books of the Tables of the Planets), and from these writings, a slightly improved version of al-Zarqali's tables was published as the *Alfonsine Tables*, and it was this set of Tables (also known as ephemerides) which was used by all of the European explorers of the 15th Century.

The Dome

In 1475, Paolo Toscanelli installed a bronze plate into the lantern above the Dome of the *Santa Maria del Fiore* Cathedral.[6] This plate is actually an astronomical instrument known as a *gnomon*, which tracks the sun's position in the sky like a sundial and shows the length of the calendar year. Every year, on June 21st, crowds of tourists visit the Cathedral to witness an event where a circle of light is projected from the sun through a uniquely placed hole in the gnomon to fill a marble disk on the chapel's floor precisely at the moment of the summer solstice.

Toscanelli's gnomon, however, was no mere parlor trick. The gnomon allowed Toscanelli to make more precise measurements as to the position and movement of the sun than any previous scientific instrument up to that time. In those years, prior to the invention of either the Dutch or Kepler telescope, the gnomon of the Flor-

---

4. The *lateen sail* design of the caravel made it the first ship capable of tacking *into* the wind and being able to maneuver on the open sea. The carrick included the lateen sail, but subsumed it within a three-masted design that included a minimum of six different sails, all of which had a separate function. It had great speed and maneuverability.

---

5. The first to solve the problem of determining longitude, at least partially, was Amerigo Vespucci (see below).
6. Some sources date this as early as 1468.

ence Cathedral was the most advanced astronomical device in the world. When comparing this precise mapping with the position of the stars, the implications for seafaring navigation were enormous.

Using the data he collected, Toscanelli corrected all the previous knowledge on the solstices and equinoxes, officially fixed with precision the date of Easter, and then proceeded to correct and improve the Alfonsine Tables.

Toscanelli's observations of projections from the top of the dome of Florence gave impetus to the genesis of a new science. Beyond coastal navigation, emerged the rebirth of astronomical navigation.

Brunelleschi's Heirs

Paolo Toscanelli, Nicholas of Cusa, and Fernão Martins de Roriz worked together throughout the entirety of their adult lives. Fernão Martins, a Canon at the Lisbon Cathedral and a relative and private counselor to Portuguese King Afonso V, was a longtime friend and collaborator of Nicholas of Cusa, and he was featured as one of the main interlocutors in Cusa's *Tetralogue on the Not-Other* (*Tetralogus de Non Aliud*). It is known that the three men frequently met at the house of Cusa at S. Pietro in Vincoli in Rome, and Fernão Martins, together with Toscanelli, would later sign, on Aug. 6, 1464, the last will and testament of Nicolas of Cusa; a few days later, they both would attend Cusa's funeral.

It was out of the partnership of these three men that the "New World" project emanated. It was not that they knew what would be discovered, because a discovery, by its very nature can not be predicted, but they knew that a new discovery, a new leap for mankind, was an imperative.

This was a time of "Confrontation between the Old and the New." By the latter part of the 15th Century, the dynamic of oligarchism was resurgent in Italy and throughout Europe. This would be borne out with the establishment of the Inquisition in Spain in 1480, the overthrow of the Florentine Republic in 1512, the Sack of Rome in 1527, the reactionary Council of Trent from 1545 to 1563, and ultimately the establishment of the new Venetian model with the coming to power of Paolo Sarpi in 1588. If the spark of the Renaissance were to survive and move forward, a new discovery, a new po-

Right: Graphic showing the gnomon installed in the Dome of the Santa Maria del Fiore Cathedral by Paolo Toscanelli. The gnomon projects the Sun's rays, every year at the moment of the Summer solstice, on a marble disk on the floor (below).

tentiality, was a necessity.

This fifty-year-long project of discovery was based in the Florentine Republic. Toscanelli, his correspondent Christopher Columbus, and the pupils of Toscanelli and Giorgio Antonio Vespucci, including Amerigo Vespucci and Lorenzo di Pierfrancesco de' Medici, would lead it.

The Correspondence

At some point, in early 1474, Fernão Martins wrote a letter to Toscanelli on the subject of a possible trans-Atlantic voyage. The exact date of the letter and its precise content are not known, because the letter is now lost. What is known is that Toscanelli replied on June 25 that year, sending to Martins a detailed proposal for a westward voyage, including a navigational map he had drawn for crossing the Atlantic. Martins presented the proposal and map to the Portuguese King Afonso V, but the king expressed no interest in the project.

That same year, in Lisbon, Christopher Columbus

learned of Toscanelli's proposal from Martins, and he wrote to Toscanelli seeking advice. Toscanelli responded with at least two letters, the first of which contained a copy of the map he had sent to Martins, but the full extent of this correspondence will never be known because none of the original documents survive.

When Columbus eventually sailed in 1492 he took a very small collection of books with him. The one which he studied most intensely was *Historia Rerum Ubique Gestarum* by Enea Silvio Piccolomini (Pope Pius II), a friend and ally of Nicholas of Cusa. The margins of this book are filled with copious notes in Columbus's handwriting, and in one of the blank pages, Columbus drew a reproduction of the Toscanelli Map.

There are also indications, from several sources, that Columbus took with him the newer versions of the Alfonsine Tables (the new tables of ephemerides) that had been improved by Toscanelli through the use of the gnomon at the *Dome* in Florence.

It must be stated here—both to warn against any attempt to diminish the personal role of Columbus, as well as to honor his courage and extraordinary skill as a navigator—that Christopher Columbus was no automaton who simply plugged in coordinates mapped by Toscanelli. Toscanelli's map was flawed, and his projected distances were off. At the same time, although Toscanelli posited that such a westward voyage were possible, there is a vast gulf between the concept of a possible discovery and the personal action required to fulfill it.

Columbus and Berardi

Armed with Toscanelli's documents, Columbus twice—in 1485 and 1488—petitioned the Portuguese monarchy for sponsorship in a westward voyage, but was turned down both times. He also turned to Spain, and on May 1, 1486 obtained an audience with Ferdinand II of Aragon and Isabella I of Castile. There, too, Columbus' proposal was rejected, but there were some in Spain ready to back him, so for the next six years Columbus continued to lobby his case at the Spanish capital. During this time Columbus also dispatched his brother Bartholomew to the court of Henry VII of England to inquire whether the English crown might sponsor his expedition, but also without success.

Eventually, in April, 1492, the Spanish monarchs aquiesced to Columbus' proposal, and he set sail on Aug. 3, 1492. Later voyages took place in 1493, 1498 and 1502.

The romantic myth is that Queen Isabella was so inspired by Columbus' vision she pawned her jewels, thus financing the first expedition. Although such a notion makes for a good Hollywood movie, that story is entirely apocryphal. It is certain that the Spanish Crown authorized the voyage and provided some monetary backing, but the main financing for the voyage came from a man named Giannotto di Lorenzo Berardi, a Florentine in the employment of Lorenzo di Pierfrancesco de' Medici, and the Director of the Spanish branch of the Medici Bank in Seville. Berardi's partners in financing Columbus' first expedition included the Florentines Giovanni Alberto Giraldini and Bernardo Scarlatti, the latter of whom was a close associate of Machiavelli's ally *Gonfalonier* Piero Soderini.

Berardi and the Medici Bank would go on to provide almost the entirety of the financing for Columbus' second expedition, and after Berardi's death in 1495, management of the Medici Bank passed into the hands of Amerigo Vespucci who organized another group of Florentine businessmen, including Francisco Cataino, Gaspar de Spinola, and Francisco de Riberole, to finance Columbus' Third Voyage. By this point, the Spanish Monarchy had become so disenchanted with Columbus, that when he returned from his third voyage, he, together with his brothers, were arrested and imprisoned.

Columbus and Vespucci

The 28-year old Amerigo Vespucci met Christopher Columbus in 1488, when Lorenzo di Pierfrancesco sent Vespucci to Seville to check into the operations of the Medici Bank located there. Vespucci remained in Seville for two years, then went back to Florence, but he returned to Seville in 1493 to become the co-director of the Bank, working under Berardi.

Earlier, in 1483, after the death of Toscanelli one year earlier, Vespucci had been taken into the household of Lorenzo di Pierfrancesco and appointed the general manager of all of Lorenzo's business and commercial interests in Florence.

While Amerigo was still in Florence, between 1490 and 1493, Berardi used the funds of Pierfrancesco's bank to fund Columbus' first voyage. After 1493, Vespucci and Berardi became the primary financial backers of Columbus' second and third voyages. Berardi and Vespucci handled all of Columbus' business affairs in Seville and equipped and outfitted his ships.

Top: The carrack Santa Maria*. Above, left to right: A portrait of a man said to be Christopher Columbus, by Sebastiano del Piombo; Amerigo Vespucci; and Lorenzo di Pierfrancesco de' Medici.*

In truth, Columbus and Vespucci were collaborators and friends, and Vespucci lived in Columbus' home during 1505 and 1506. Perhaps the best witness to their relationship is Columbus himself, who after his return from his fourth voyage met with Vespucci and gave him a letter to deliver to his son, Diego. The letter says, in part:

I talked with the bearer of this letter, Amerigo Vespucci, who is going to court where he has been summoned by King Ferdinand in connection with matters of navigation. It has always been his desire to give me pleasure; he is a man of good will; fortune has proved contrary to him; he has not profited from his labors as justice would demand. He is acting in my behalf, moved by a great desire to do something which shall be to my benefit if it lies within his power.

IV. Amerigo Vespucci and his Voyages

Christopher Columbus, Piero Soderini, Leonardo da Vinci, Amerigo Vespucci, Lorenzo di Pierfrancesco de' Medici, and Niccolo Machiavelli. Five of these six men were from Florence. Four were born between 1450 and 1454, and the other two in 1463 and 1469, with Machiavelli being the youngest. They were of one generation.

All of these men, with the exception of the too-young Machiavelli, were associated with Toscanelli, some very closely, and three of them—Soderini, Pierfrancesco and Vespucci—had been students of Toscanelli's partner Giorgio Antonio Vespucci.

As a youth, Amerigo had been personally tutored by Toscanelli and spent many hours at Toscanelli's home. He had full access to Toscanelli's maps and scientific instruments, and he was there at the time of the Toscanelli-Columbus correspondence in 1474. Although,

Vespucci lived in Berardi's home, and this residence became the headquarters for Columbus when he was in Seville. Columbus' Second Voyage was mapped out in Berardi's parlor, and one can only imagine the discussions which took place between Columbus and Vespucci during those years.

Vespucci has been routinely defamed in history books and accused of conspiring to steal Columbus' fame. Ralph Waldo Emerson, the dean of the American "transcendentalists," had this to say of him, "Strange that broad America must wear the name of a thief. Amerigo Vespucci, the pickle-dealer at Seville, whose highest naval rank was boatswain's mate in an expedition that never sailed, managed in this lying world to... baptize half the world with his own dishonest name."

later, Amerigo would work for more than a decade running business and financial affairs for Pierfrancesco, his character was formed in the years prior to 1482 studying and working under Toscanelli.

Lorenzo di Pierfrancesco de' Medici was the cousin of Lorenzo the Magnificent (Lorenzo di Piero de' Medici), but he was also his political rival. After Il Magnifico's death in 1492, Pierfrancesco played a key role in overthrowing Lorenzo di Piero's son and establishing the Republic. The Vespucci family were among his closest political allies.

It was Pierfrancesco, together with the Vespuccis, who were the primary backers of Machiavelli's political career. Machiavelli's closest ally was *Gonfalonier* Piero Soderini, the head of the Republic. Between 1499 and 1505, when Amerigo wrote a series of letters describing his voyages across the Atlantic, all of these letters were sent to either Piero Soderini or Lorenzo di Pierfrancesco, the former students of Giorgio Antonio Vespucci.

After the death of Lorenzo the Magnificent, Pierfrancesco also inherited control over the Medici banking establishment and all of its branches. He deployed Amerigo to Seville to take control of the branch there, and it was through the Medici bank that Columbus's voyages were financed.

The Voyages

In his letters,[7] Amerigo Vespucci describes four voyages he made across the Atlantic between 1497 and 1503. This is much disputed by the anti-Vespucci clique, but there is no legitimate reason to deny the truth of his reports. After 1504 he was hailed as the "Prince of Scientific Navigation" in both Spain and Portugal by kings and sea captains alike, accolades which certainly would not have been bestowed on someone who, in Emerson's words, was the "pickle-dealer" of Seville.

There is even marginal information from third-party sources, indicating that Vespucci may have made two additional trans-Atlantic voyages, in 1505 and 1507,

---

7. It is important to understand the role of "letters" during this period. At a time when there were no newspapers, letters were the indispensable source of news from around the world. Except for those most personal of nature, most letters were recopied by hand over and over again, and circulated quite freely. These were known as "familiar" letters, and the authors of these letters consciously designed their messages to reach a much broader audience.

but there is no mention of this by Vespucci in any of his writings that exist today, so the truth may never be known.

One of the charges made against Vespucci is that, unlike Columbus, he did not command any of those voyages, and, in fact, only piloted a single ship on one occasion. This is true, but it is an empty accusation. Vespucci was not, by training or inclination, a sea captain. He was educated by Toscanelli. He was a cosmographer, an astronomer, a map-maker, and he became the greatest navigator of his time. He was, in short, a scientist.

* * * * *

The first two of Vespucci's voyages were carried out under the Spanish flag. His third and fourth voyages were for Portugal. Of particular note are the second and third voyages, both of which he describes in letters to Lorenzo di Pierfrancesco.

On the second voyage, Vespucci traveled in a group of four ships under the command of Alonso de Ojeda. At some point, either in Guyana or at the Canary Islands, Vespucci's vessel separated from the others, with Ojeda exploring the coastline of Venezuela and Vespucci continuing southward to Brazil. Vespucci discovered the mouth of the Amazon River. He then turned around and explored the Orinoco River in Venezuela which had previously been discovered by Columbus. He visited Trinidad and then rejoined Ojeda in Hispaniola, where they set sail for Spain.

It was on this expedition, on Aug. 23, 1499, that Vespucci discovered a method to determine longitude celestially, and he writes in detail as to how he arrived at this discovery in a letter to Lorenzo di Pierfrancesco de' Medici. More will be said on this below.

Shortly after returning to Spain in 1500, Vespucci left Seville, and traveled to the court of King Manuel I in Lisbon. There he was commissioned as the chief navigator on an expedition of three caravels, under the command of Gonçalo Coelho which returned to Brazil in 1501.

Upon reaching Brazil, Vespucci's ship broke off from the others and headed south. He spent the next ten months south of the equator, exploring the entire coastline of Argentina and traveling almost 2,500 miles. Vespucci's ship ventured as far as 53° south latitude, at Tierra del Fuego, 18 years before Magellan reached that spot. Vespucci was the first to explore the Amazon

River, and the first to discover the Rio de la Plata.[8]

During this third voyage, Vespucci continued his astronomical investigations, mapping the constellation Crux or the Southern Cross, and also Alpha and Beta Centauri. Crux is hardly visible from the Northern Hemisphere, while the latter two stars had been known to the Greeks, but due to gradual precession they had dropped below the European horizon and had been forgotten in the mist of time. The position of these stars and constellations proved to be a valuable navigational aid to future expeditions.

It was on this voyage that Vespucci became convinced, through a combination of geographical exploration and astronomical observations, that a new continent had been discovered, that this land-mass was neither an island, nor part of Asia. In a letter to Lorenzo di Pierfrancesco he dubbed this continent *Mundus Novus* (the New World).

Navigation: a Willful Act of Discovery

In the letters which Amerigo writes to both Piero Soderini and Lorenzo di Pierfrancesco de' Medici, he describes in great detail his astronomical and scientific observations.

On his second voyage Vespucci makes an intensive study of how to determine longitudinal position at sea. Previously, navigation was based on using the phases of the moon to determine tides, using the meridian altitude of the sun to steer by day, and the positions of Ursa Major and Ursa Minor to steer by night. Vespucci became the first to determine longitude at sea, by making precise measurements of the conjunction of the moon with the planets and constellations.

In a letter to Lorenzo, Vespucci writes:

As to longitude, I declare that I found so much difficulty in determining it that I was put to great pains to ascertain the east-west distance I had covered. The final result of my labors was that I found nothing better to do than to watch for and take observations at night of the conjunction of one planet with another, and especially of the conjunction of the moon with the other planets, because the moon is swifter in her course than any other planet. I compared my observations with an almanac. After I had made experiments many nights, one night, the twenty-third of August 1499, there was a conjunction of the moon with Mars, which according to the almanac was to occur at midnight or a half hour before. I found that ... at midnight Mars's position was three and a half degrees to the east.

During Vespucci's third voyage his ship spent ten months below the equator, and he conducted extensive studies of the southern constellations. In another letter to Lorenzo he recounts the many sleepless nights he devoted to the examination of the Southern Cross, and the many laborious calculations which he entered into, quoting from his favorite poet:

Each star of the other pole, night now beheld
And ours so low, that from the ocean floor
It rose not ...
(Dante, *Purgatorio*, Canto xxvi)

It is in this voyage, based on precise measurements of longitude, that Vespucci determines that the sphere of the earth is much larger than previously thought, and it was from these astronomical observations, rather than merely the size of the South American land mass, that he concluded a new continent had been discovered.

As he says in his letter to Lorenzo: "We reached a new land which we discovered to be the mainland... I reached the region of the antipodes, which according to my navigation is the fourth part of the world."[9]

Based on this voyage, Vespucci is recognized as the greatest navigator of his time. By the end of his voyages in 1504 Vespucci's explorations were more extensive than any other mariner up to that time, and his scientific readings were more accurate.

Afterwards

In 1620, only 93 years after Machiavelli's death, forty-one passengers on board the Mayflower signed a Compact in which they committed to "combine our-

---

8. It is interesting to note that while the Florentine Vespucci was the first European to explore the entirety of the eastern South American coastline, it was another Florentine, Giovanni da Verrazano, in 1524, who first explored the length of the North American coast, from Florida to Newfoundland, on a voyage backed by the French King Francis I, the same monarch who was the benefactor of Leonardo da Vinci, during the final years of his life.

---

9. It was commonly held, at that time, that there were three parts to the world: Europe, Asia, and Africa.

V. Man's Destiny

Taking as a whole everything which has been presented up to this point, ask yourself this question: Is this not mankind's mission? Is this not *our* destiny and that of our posterity? Or—are we to eternally exist, from generation to generation, in a way that would bring a knowing smile to the lips of the British Queen and her progeny: grunting and rooting in the muck, amidst the daily pleasures of an entropic culture, in the manner of pathetic feral creatures?

In 1966 Krafft Ehricke addressed this question in a paper he authored entitled "Solar Exploration."[10] He states:

The challenge of distance and worlds beyond has always exerted a magic influence on man, causing him to overcome even the most powerful fears, born out of the superstitions of his time and to plunge into the unknown. No matter how this drive is rationalized by establishing a causality with certain apparent utilities at that time, there remains an important basic influence which is emotional and which is rooted in the deep-seated obsession to penetrate the mysteries of nature and to absorb them into a system of human understanding. This unquenchable thirst for knowledge and understanding is perhaps the third of man's basic drives. While he shares two others—hunger and sex—with all life on earth, the third is his alone and sets him apart from the other creatures as being endowed with a mind that must forever

Above: Pilgrims signing—on arrival in the New World—the Mayflower Compact, an agreement to establish a political entity. Right: The Saugus Iron Works, founded in Massachusetts in 1646 by John Winthrop.

selves together into a civil body politic." Ten years later John Winthrop and his allies established the great Commonwealth in Massachusetts Bay, founded on the principle of the Common Good.

Between 1630 and 1688, under Winthrop's leadership, Massachusetts enacted measures for public education and internal improvements. They established a credit system, through the Pine Tree Shilling, and used it to finance science and industry.

Winthrop's son, John Winthrop Jr., created the Saugus Iron Works, and corresponded with Gottfried Leibniz, and his library included the works of Machiavelli, Kepler, Jean Bodin, and Erasmus. Such was the potential unleashed by the heroes of the 15th Century.

---

10. *Space Age in Fiscal Year 2001*, An American Astronautical Society Publication, 1967.

feed on the unknown or die. The unknown is the preferred challenge after all, if compared with the business of coercing and killing his own kind. Crossing established frontiers of the known world, mentally or physically, is mankind's way of maturing and is one of the few fundamental causes of terrible crises and of true and lasting happiness known. Man entered space as an earth-oriented being. Now, space begins to transform him into a cosmically-oriented being with a broader and more mature outlook at his own small planet and the problems of living on it.

People often ask, "Why did the Renaissance collapse into the religious wars and barbarism of the 16th and 17th Centuries?" This is the wrong question to ask. No amount of exploring the role of the Venetian or Dutch Empires or the various oligarchical conspiracies will provide an answer. The better question is "How does the human species progress from one generation to the next?" What is necessary to ensure a better future era from the one which is passing from the scene? This is where the Imperative for Discovery comes into play. The discovery of New Worlds, New Universal Principles, New Potentialities—these are the prerequisites for human survival.

Furthermore, it is not enough to merely recognize that imperative. Each new generation—and key individuals within that generation—must willfully act to make those necessary discoveries, often under conditions of crisis. That is the historic responsibility which must be met. No society, no culture, now matter how great, is of the nature of a self-perpetuating machine, and simply "contemplating" the greatness of previous cultures is a habitat for foolish romantics.

Revolutionary Evolution

In 2015, Lyndon LaRouche addressed this question of the willful character of human evolution in the following way:

> I can tell you one thing, that the generation of the people of the United States, since the beginning of the Twentieth Century to the present time, has been one of degeneration!
>
> Now, what we've got to do, is we've got to reverse that problem. We've got to eliminate the factor of degeneration which is the characteristic of the Twentieth Century and beyond. And Bertrand Russell, of course, is the typical agent who typifies that degeneracy. We are living in the United States under a degenerate culture. Now we have to end that degenerate culture, by replacing it with a higher, a proper generation of culture,—as Brunelleschi did in his lifetime. Brunelleschi did things that nobody else was able to do, among all the people around him. He's a remarkable genius,—and it's the remarkable factor of genius among great minds,—and his accomplishments were immense. And that's the way you have to look at it.
>
> We have to take our children, we have to take those we're educating, and we have to get them to see what they can do, the miracles that they can develop and create as a result of their passion for the progress of mankind.
>
> There is no such thing as an evolutionary process of development of human culture. There are effects which occur at certain times. But then, suddenly, the whole culture collapses, vanishes, it's slaughtered. Then later, somebody else arrives, stimulates something new, and gives mankind another chance at progress.
>
> And our job is to understand this question of progress, and progress is not an evolutionary process. *It's always a revolutionary process, it is never evolutionary!* And everybody who's sitting around waiting for a revolutionary process is just kidding themselves. *A revolution of that type has to be an act of genius*, which comes as if from nowhere. But that's the way mankind succeeds. And I'm looking for people who will do that kind of work, and become the geniuses who cause the future to be reborn again.[11]

Create or perish. As we look back at the magnificence of what was accomplished 500 years ago, how shall our descendants, 500 years into the future, judge our own actions?

---

11. "The Principle of Brunelleschi," by Lyndon H. LaRouche, Jr., *Executive Intelligence Review*, December 11, 2015.

Every Day Counts In Today's Showdown To Save Civilization

That's why you need EIR's **Daily Alert Service**, a strategic overview compiled with the input of Lyndon LaRouche, and delivered to your email 5 days a week.

For example: On Jan. 7, EIR's Daily Alert featured the British hand behind the pattern of global provocations toward war. Of special note is British Intelligence's role in instigating the Saudi Kingdom's attempt to set off a Sunni-Shia war. This religious war has been the intent of British strategy since the Blair-Bush attack on Iraq in 2003.

We also uniquely update you regularly on the progress toward the release of the suppressed 28 pages of the Congressional Inquiry on 9/11, which would expose the Saudi role.

Every edition highlights the reality of the impending financial crash/bail-in policies that would realize the British goal of mass depopulation.

This is intelligence you need to act on, if we are going to survive as a nation and a species. Can you really afford to be without it?

THURSDAY, JANUARY 7, 2016

Volume 2, Number 97

EIR Daily Alert Service

P.O. BOX 17390, WASHINGTON, DC 20041-0390

- British Crown Pushing War and Genocide in 2016
- Financial Mudslide Goes On; Monetarist Tyranny Gloats over Bail-Ins
- Moody's Downgrades Portugal's Novo Banco
- Puerto Rico's Default: It's Every Vulture for Himself
- Wide Glass-Steagall Debate Set Off Again by Sanders Speech
- MI6 Mouthpiece Evans-Pritchard Touts Persian Gulf Chaos
- North Korea Tests a Miniaturized Hydrogen Bomb
- Uighur Terrorists Found in Indonesia
- Foreign Investors Are Flocking In to China

EDITORIAL

British Crown Pushing War and Genocide in 2016

THE HERRHAUSEN METHOD

A Serious Challenge to the Genocidal Trans-Atlantic System

by Rainer Apel

July 30—On July 12, Helga Zepp-LaRouche issued an urgent appeal, "Deutsche Bank Must be Saved for the Sake of World Peace," which called for a government recapitalization of that derivatives-laden bank, conditional on its immediately reversing its policies back to those of its murdered former Chairman Alfred Herrhausen. This campaign of Lyndon and Helga LaRouche is continuing and intensifying, and is finding a growing response internationally. What is at stake is either an uncontrolled world financial blowout leading to war,—or an orderly reorganization towards recovery.

The chief speaker (equivalent to Chairman) of Deutsche Bank's board, Alfred Herrhausen, was killed in his car on his way to the bank by a remote-control bomb, on the morning of Nov. 30, 1989. The assassins have never been found or identified. The official version, instantly given to the press after the incident, is that he was killed by a team of the "third generation" of the infamous Baader-Meinhof gang (RAF, *Rote Armee Fraktion*), but that was never proven; it was also never proven that such a "third generation" even existed.

Crucial pieces of evidence have mysteriously disappeared during the past 26 years—including the wreckage of the car, whose availability would be important to determine in a renewed investigation, what kind of bomb was actually used in the assault, and whether that could provide leads into other circles that might have

Foto: Ruhr Initiative Group

The First press conference of the "initiative Ruhrgebiet," promoting the reindustrialization of the Ruhr region in Germany, on Feb. 15, 1989. Shown here (from left): Cardinal Franz Hengsbach, Jürgen Gramke, Alfred Herrhausen, Rudolf von Bennigsen-Foerder and Friedhelm Gieske.

had an interest in killing Herrhausen.

It is widely known that particularly during the period between the big Wall Street Crash of October 1987, and the day of his assassination, Herrhausen had made himself many enemies in the trans-Atlantic world of banking and finance, with his unconventional proposals for solutions to the international debt crisis, and for economic-financial cooperation of the West with the Soviet Union—proposals that posed a serious challenge to the principles of financial policies in the western trans-Atlantic system—principles which have had increasingly genocidal effects.

Like John F. Kennedy and his brother Robert, Alfred Herrhausen was not murdered for anything that he had done (still less for anything he had said), but for what he threatened to do in the future. This threat was reflected in his public statements. In our July 22 issue, *EIR* quoted on page 20, from the speech Herrhausen was scheduled to give in New York on December 4, 1989, four days after his assassination, with its straight challenge to destructive trans-Atlantic banking methods. Two earlier statements which Herrhausen had given in June and September, already contained the core components of what he would have said in New York, had he not been assassinated.

Herrhausen's Answers to the Crisis

In an essay headlined, "The Time Has Come —Debt Crisis at a Turning Point," published by Germany's leading business daily *Handelsblatt* on June 30, 1989, Herrhausen denounced the debt policies of particularly the U.S. banks. Not only were they useless, he wrote, but they were only worsening the debtor nations' situation as well as that of the creditor banks themselves. Instead, the only measures that would work were general debt write-offs of up to 70%, cuts in interest of up to 50% for five years, a grace period of five years granted to all debtors, and an extension of the maturity of loans to 25 or 30 years.

This approach, he insisted, would "enable the said (debtor) nations to reassign considerable resources that so far had been used to serve the debt, to instead be used for such purposes as would serve the recovery of their domestic economies." Herrrhausen added that what debtor nations really needed was not fresh money— that is, new debt—but "it would be better to say they need resources." The net effect of this "resources reallocation could, during the first five years, be bigger than

[all] the fresh money injections they have requested so far."

Herrhausen did not reference it directly, but what he proposed was the approach generally taken in the London Debt Agreement of 1952, that created enormous relief for postwar Western Germany to get back on its feet, and not collapse under the weight of the piled-up old debt. That Agreement had been negotiated by Deutsche Bank's longtime Chairman Hermann Josef Abs—the outstanding constructive banker who also played a role in promoting the career of a promising young banker with the name of Alfred Herrhausen.

On another occasion, an extensive press briefing on Sept. 25, 1989, at the World Bank's autumn meeting in Washington, D.C., Herrhausen presented the same arguments, pointing out that he very much hoped that other banks would follow the example of Deutsche Bank as a "debt reduction bank," as it had shown itself to be in several cases of developing-sector debtor nations. Herrhausen warned that the unresolved payments problems of the debtor nations, along with problems resulting from debt imbalances in the United States itself and in Europe, posed a systemic risk, whose dimensions had been understated for too long. It was high time to act, and to do so in a constructive way, Herrhausen insisted. At the same time, unrest in the Soviet Union despite its reforms, along with nationality frictions and "escalated conflicts erupting from that," could lead to problems particularly in the Soviet Bloc, with negative repercussions for all Eastern Europe. Herrhausen proposed for unstable Poland in particular, the creation of a special new bank in Warsaw, an "Agency for Reconstruction," which unlike the current banking practices of the West, would make sure that new loans to the Polish economy would be used for clearly-defined industrial development projects, just as the Marshall Plan money of the United States was used for well-defined reconstruction in Germany and Europe after World War II. There must also be a substantial cut in the high foreign debt of Poland.

With that, Herrhausen had addressed in his own words what Lyndon H. LaRouche had laid out in his own historic speech at the Kempinski Hotel in Berlin, on Oct. 12, 1988. That speech was being studied by many policy-makers and bankers in the months following, and one may assume that Herrhausen had the text on his desk at some point as well.

Is the Battle for Aleppo Now a Turning Point In the Syria War?

by Carl Osgood

July 31—On July 27, the Syrian military command announced that it had completed the encirclement of the rebel-held portion of Aleppo, the largest city in Syria and once its commercial capital, by completely cutting the Castello Road, the last route into that part of the city to the northwest for the armed opposition groups. By doing so, the Syrian army, with backing from the Russian Aerospace Forces contingent deployed in Latakia, has made the positions of the terrorist groups untenable.

Footage released July 30, 2016, of Syrian refugees who left the parts of Aleppo occupied by ISIS, via humanitarian corridors.

At the same time, the Syrian government, in concert with the Russian military, is moving to rapidly conclude the situation rather than digging in for a lengthy siege. The July 27 military announcement triggered an uproar from international humanitarian aid NGOs, which warned that starvation for the 250,000 civilians estimated to still be in that part of the city would soon follow.

Russian Defense Minister Sergei Shoigu and the Syrian government, in a move that was likely pre-planned for some time, announced on July 28 the commencement of a large scale humanitarian relief operation. "We have been continuously appealing to the opposing sides for reconciliation, but every time insurgents broke the 'silence regime,' shelled inhabited areas, and attacked positions of the government troops. All this caused a bad humanitarian situation in Aleppo city and its suburbs," Shoigu said at the Russian Defense Ministry on July 28. "Therefore, in accord with the decree of the President of the Russian Federation, the Minister of Defense gave orders to start a large-scale humanitarian operation aimed at providing assistance to the civilian population of Aleppo city in cooperation with the Syrian government."

International humanitarian organizations operating in Syria have been invited to join the operation. Three humanitarian corridors were opened for civilians and for fighters who decide to lay down their weapons, while a fourth corridor was opened on the Castello Road for armed militants to withdraw. On July 31, Lieutenant-General Sergey Chvarkov, the head of the Russian reconciliation center at the Latakia airbase, announced that four more corridors would be opened.

Shoigu also announced that under orders from Russian President Vladimir Putin, in response to a personal request from U.S. Secretary of State John Kerry, Deputy

cc/Mohammad Reza Jofar

Some of the Syrian Army troops who were involved in breaking the several-year-long siege of of the pro-government Shi'ite villages of Nubl and Al-Zahra (combined population 35,000) in Aleppo province on Feb. 4, 2016.

Chief of the Main Operational Directorate General Stanislav Gadjimagomedov was going to Geneva with a group of experts, in order to develop joint measures with the United States aimed at the stabilization of situation near Aleppo.

A Work-in-Progress

At the same time, Syrian President Bashar al Assad has signed a decree granting amnesty for members of armed groups who turn themselves in to the competent authorities and lay down their weapons, and those who set free, in a safe manner, persons they have kidnapped. According to Sputnik, the decree says that "Armed fugitives hiding from justice shall be exempt from liability if they surrender and hand over their weapons to the competent judicial authorities or the police within three months from the date of this decree's publication."

The next step will be restarting the Syrian peace negotiations. Russia's ambassador to the UN in Geneva, Alexey Borodavkin, reported on July 28 that President Assad has sent an invitation to UN Envoy Staffan De Mistura's deputy, Ramzy Ezzeldin Ramzy, to discuss ways for possible political settlement of the crisis in the country. "Only a political transition process, with participation of the moderate opposition in reforming state institutions, will allow achievement of a ceasefire and settlement of the inter-Syrian conflict," Borodavkin said.

In remarks on July 29 reported by the Russian Defense Ministry, Deputy Defense Minister Anatoly Antonov expressed cautious optimism that the humanitarian initiative might work. He emphasized that the Russian military is doing everything possible to relieve the humanitarian situation in Aleppo. Indeed, this is the sole focus of the operation, and the Russian foreign and defense ministries have already sent out appeals to foreign counterparts and organizations to join the effort. "The first response is quite positive," Antonov said.

"The organizations 'Doctors Without Borders' and ICRC, as well as the office of the Special Envoy of the UN Secretary-General for Syria Staffan de Mistura have shown interest in the operation." At the same time, he noted that "the reaction of some media agencies and political figures, who have seen a disguised plan in the Russian actions, is surprising." This is exclusively humanitarian, but the Russian military, he said, "will not admit the flow of arms, under any circumstances, to the regions controlled by the militants."

While it's not clear what's happening on the ground with the corridors, what is clear is that the operation remains a work in progress. Military experts consulted by Sputnik "are warning against too much optimism. Encirclement, they note, does not mean victory." The kind of urban warfare that an assault on the remaining rebel-held portions of Aleppo would imply, is difficult, dangerous, and absorbs a great deal of military effort and resources. This is why, one expert surmised, Damascus and Moscow are instead trying to convince the militants to leave. "If this occurs, organized resistance will not be possible, and the city can be taken." It remains to be seen, however, whether or not this will happen.

Eurasian Land-Bridge Extends Its Reach

by Ramtanu Maitra

July 31—Two important developments in the last week of July promise advances in the Eurasian Land-Bridge's connectivity between East and South Asia with Europe, via Central Asia and Iran. While these and related developments are in progress, the developed nations in Europe and North America, mired in self-inflicted financial hara-kiri, are encountering a backlash against their most disturbing regime change policy—a policy that has given birth to a most violent form of global terrorism now completely overwhelming the western policymakers. The Land-Bridge developments are also blossoming in a region—where a majority of the world's population lives—whose peoples have suffered centuries of colonial rule and post-colonial control through, for example, financial warfare manipulations, leaving the region without development and often desperately short of even the basic infrastructures needed for survival.

On July 27, the first Inner Mongolia container train to Astana, capital city of Kazakstan, was flagged off from Baotou, Inner Mongolia, initiating the first train service between the two points. Inner Mongolia is an Autonomous Region of China.

Perhaps at the same moment, the Governor of Russia's Astrakhan Region, Alexander Zhilkin, was in Iran, proposing the creation of a Russia-Iran-India unified transport and logistics company to operate the trans-Caspian maritime branch of the International North-South Transport Corridor (INSTC). The INSTC will run from India to Iran, Russia, and Europe. The Astrakhan Region is on the Caspian. It lies astride the Volga River and the Volga's delta, across the Caspian from Iran. Zhilkin's proposal was in the news in both countries on July 28.

Zhilkin met with representatives of the National Iranian Oil Company and with Iran's Deputy Minister of Industry, Mines, and Trade, Mojtaba Khosrowtaj, to discuss creating the company, with Indian participation. Commenting on Zhilkin's proposal, Konstantin Zavrazhin writing for the *Russia & India Report* (RIR)

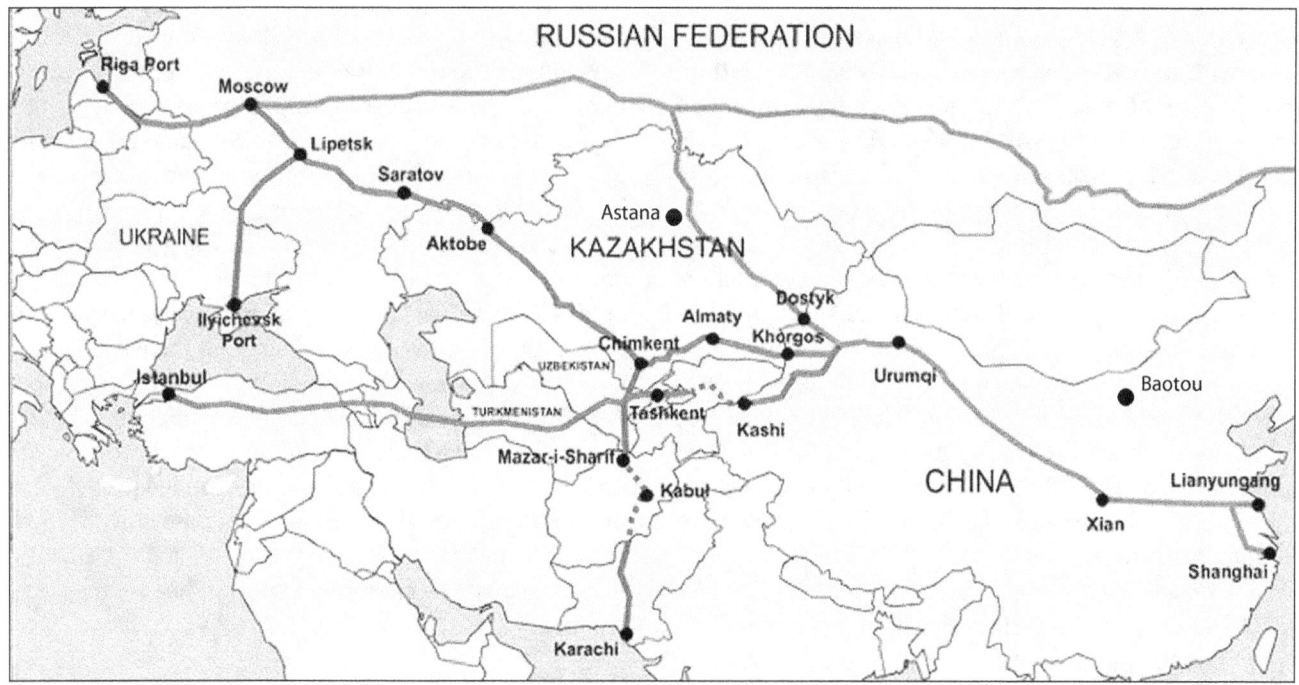

The first two rail routes through Kazakstan, linking China with Europe, Russia, and Central and South Asia, are shown here, with border crossings at Dostyk and Khorgos. The new, third route connects Baotou in China with the Kazakh capital, Astana.

of July 28, said "this would ensure that the representative of each of the countries would be responsible for their link in the overall structure of the corridor."

Third China-Kazakh Rail Link

The freight train with 41 container cars, flagged off July 27 from Jiuyuan Logistics Park in Baotou, Inner Mongolia, is to traverse the 4,332 kilometers of western China in eight days to enter Kazakstan. Its last stop on the Chinese side will be Alashankou railway station before it is connected to the Atasu-Astana rail line to reach the Kazakh capital, Astana. According to *China Daily* July 29, the Baotou-Astana service, dubbed the 21st Century Silk Road, will go along the Baotou-Lanzhou, Linhe-Hami, and Lanzhou-Xinjiang railway lines before it arrives at Alashankou railway station. The container cars carried building materials and other commodities. On its return journey, the train will carry goods such as mineral resources, according to a Hohhot (Inner Mongolia) Railway Bureau official, Xinhua reported on July 27. The City of Baotou in Inner Mongolia is in turn linked by rail with Beijing, almost due east, 820 kilometers away.

Jiuyuan Logistics Park in Baotou was established earlier this year, combining an online goods trading platform and a warehouse to serve as a logistics center for the chemical, coal, steel, nonferrous metal, and grains industries. In addition to its integration with the rail freight services, it integrates trade with financial services and third-party logistical services.

The Baotou-Astana Silk Road rail route is the third that links China to Kazakhstan for China's rail-based trading with Central Asia, Russia, and Europe. In December 2012, Kazakhstan completed construction of a 183-mile stretch from Zhetygen to Korgas on the Chinese border, integrating it into the existing Kazakhstan Temir Zholy national railway network and opening the second China-Europe link across its territory, supplementing the Alataw trade pass of the first China-Central Asia railway connection, John C.K. Daly of *Silk Road Reporters* said in a July 14, 2015 report. Located 670 kilometers west of Urumqi, the capital of Xinjiang province, Korgas lies 90 kilometers northwest of Yining, the principal town in China's Ili Kazakh autonomous prefecture. Daly wrote:

> Alataw is where the 6,950-mile Yuxinou (Chongqing-Xinjiang-Europe) International Railway crosses from China into Kazakhstan, travels through Russia, Belarus, and Poland, and ar-

rives in Duisburg, Germany. Cargo transportation from China to Germany began in 2011. In January-October 2012, 32 trains travelled the Yuxinou International Railway, with 2,700 20-foot containers, carrying high-value, low-volume items such as electronics. Alataw now reportedly handles 15.6 million tons of train-laden cargo a year.

By establishing these routes through Kazakhstan, Chinese exporters have succeeded in cutting at least 35 days off the 45-day maritime shipping route to Europe. Accordingly, Kazakhstan has now emerged as an important hub linking Europe, the Middle East, Asia, and Russia. In future, these rail linkages will enable greater trade between China, Kazakhstan, other members of the Commonwealth of Independent States (CIS), and Europe. With almost 12,500 miles of tracks, the Kazakh railway network, world's third biggest, uses a different rail gauge—the 1,520 millimeter track gauge used by the Russian rail network, rather than the standard gauge used by the China and Europe. Transfers of freight from one gauge to another are done by crane. Containerization makes this process more efficient.

Astrakhan's Maritime Initiative

Zhilkin's proposal for a unified transport and logistics company for INSTC trade along the route from Mumbai (India), to Bandar Abbas (Iran), Bandar Anzali on the Caspian (Iran), and over the water to Astrakhan (Russia), will doubtless bring trade-related economic development to the Astrakhan Region itself. The meeting in Iran also discussed the use of Astrakhan's Olya Port to import Iranian goods to Russia, and the opening of an Iranian trading house in Astrakhan, according to Zavrazhin's report in *RIR* report.

Astrakhan's initiative to use the Caspian Sea as another valuable arm of the INSTC is also important for all of the Caspian coastal countries. Iran, Russia, and Azerbaijan are also now actively pursuing the entirely rail-based arm, which will link the Persian Gulf port, Bandar Abbas, to Russia through Azerbaijan, along the western coast of the Caspian.[1] For Iran, of course, both arms are important, since the majority of the people in Iran live in the northern part of the country, in proximity to both routes. To make the rail-based route along the west coast of the Caspian Sea operable, a new rail line is now being

---

1. For more detail on the INSTC, see "Breakthrough on the Gulf of Oman: Big Step to Link Asia and Europe," by Ramtanu Maitra, *EIR*, June 3, 2016.

Vladimir Putin, then prime minister, with Alexander Zhilkin, Governor of the Astrakhan Region (right), visits the Astrakhan Shipbuilding Production Association in 2009.

built linking the Azerbaijani city of Astara to its Iranian cross-border counterpart, also called Astara, and the Iranian cities of Rasht and Qazvin.

Construction of the Qazvin-Rasht section was completed in 2015, but construction of the Rasht-Astara section, a challenging engineering project because of the topography, is still at an early stage—but it is making progress. Azerbaijan's Foreign Minister, Elmar Mammadyarov, in an April 7 statement, said that the linking of the Iranian and Azerbaijani rail networks will be completed this year. The estimated capacity of the railway, during the first phase, should be around 4 to 10 million tons of cargo per year, and will increase.

Russia is now working to make the Corridor operable as soon as possible. An April 7 news report of the Russian *Vzglyad*, following Russian Foreign Minister Sergei Lavrov's talks with the foreign ministers of Azerbaijan and Iran, said that—

> Lavrov has revealed that Russia has agreed to begin substantive studies on the implementation of the North-South Transport Corridor, part of which will pass along the western coast of the Caspian Sea, from Russia to Iran through Azerbaijan. "This involves working with the participation of the [different participants'] ministries of transport, which have to look at the technical and financial parameters of such a project. This also involves interaction between the customs and consular services, and we have agreed on this today," said Lavrov.

Meanwhile, Zhilkin's proposal could make at least the over-water arm of the Corridor operational within a short period of time. He is aware of New Delhi's and Tehran's interest. Indian Prime Minister Narendra Modi, while he was chief minister of India's northwestern state of Gujarat, had visited Astrakhan, met with Zhilkin, and embraced Astrakhan region as Gujarat's sister state.

The link between India and Astrakhan is, however, much older. According to Francis C. Assisi,[2] the Indian presence in Russia dates back to the 17th century. By then, Indian traders had reached as far as Isfahan in Iran, Kizlyar in the North Caucasus, and the city of Astrakhan, the Russian trading port in the Volga delta on the Caspian. The first Indians from Sindh and Multan (areas now in Pakistan) arrived in Astrakhan in 1615-1616. Surviving records show they were dealers in Astrakhan textiles, jewelry, and medicines. In 1650, Indian merchants are known to have sold their goods in Yaroslavl, not far from Moscow. Thereafter the Romanov Tsar, Alexei Mikhaylovich, invited Indian artisans to Moscow to introduce a textile industry there.

Russian Railways' Contribution

In the Russian portion of the Corridor, according to Russian Railways,[3] "the most important section for developing transit and export-import freight . . . is the 2,513 kilometers of the line Buslovskaya-Saint Petersburg-Moscow-Ryazan-Kotchetovka-Rtischevo-Saratov-Volgograd-Astrakhan. This route provides access to other parts of Russia, as well as to the Baltic states, Ukraine, and Belarus, and then on to the European railway network."

Russia's Federal Program for the Modernization of the Transport System provides for upgrading and reconstruction of the line from Astrakhan to Samur, near the border with Azerbaijan.

For the maritime branch, Russian Railways built a 50 kilometer rail spur in less than a year, linking the Port of Olya (Astrakhan) with the main route just described, which "immediately allowed the transport of up to 6 million tons of German exports" to reach Iran and the Persian Gulf by the shortest route, that is, the newly developed sea route that Astrakhan's Zhilkin is seeking to organize at the international level.

2. This historical sketch draws primarily on "The Indian Diaspora in Russia" by Francis C. Assisi.
3. See the North-South Corridor page (updated July 30) of the Russian Railways website.

www.ingramcontent.com/pod-product-compliance
Lightning Source LLC
Chambersburg PA
CBHW080325290526
45793CB00006B/1214